LIFE IS CRAP®

Published by Sellers Publishing, Inc.

161 John Roberts Road, South Portland, Maine 04106
For ordering information:
(800) 625-3386 Toll free
(207) 772-6814 Fax
Visit our Web site: www.sellerspublishing.com
E-mail: rsp@rsvp.com

ISBN: 13: 978-1-4162-0768-9

10 9 8 7 6 5 4 3 2

Printed and bound in Manitoba, Canada.

LIFE IS CRAP®

When Bad Sh*t Happens to Good People

SELLERS
PUBLISHING

PORTLAND, MAINE

Once upon a time,
not so long ago,
we thought life was pretty good,

LIFE IS CRAP®

and then we found out. . .

LIFE IS CRAP®

it wasn't.

LIFE IS CRAP®

As time went by,
the mood became darker
and darker.

LIFE IS CRAP®

But a wise person once said,

LIFE IS CRAP®

things may not always
roll your way.

LIFE IS CRAP®

Life may put a few
obstacles in your path.

COLLECTIONS HAS BEEN NOTIFIED!

PAST DUE

LIFE IS CRAP®

Your glass may not always
be half full.

OUT OF BEER

LIFE IS CRAP®

You may be
feeling undervalued.

LIFE IS CRAP®

But don't worry,
you'll always be "number one"
to somebody.

LIFE IS CRAP®

In this crazy world, things can quickly go awry.

YOU'RE FIRED

LIFE IS CRAP®

You may not always
land on your feet.

LIFE IS CRAP®

Sharks may be
circling overhead.

LIFE IS CRAP®

Bad luck may seem like
it's following you around.

LIFE IS CRAP®

The well may run dry,

LIFE IS CRAP®

but at least you'll always
have a friend.

LIFE IS CRAP®

Someone you can count on,

through good times and bad.

LIFE IS CRAP®

Life's not always fair.

10 ITEMS OR LESS

BE BE BE BE BE CHIPS

LIFE IS CRAP®

it can be a real pain.

DR. BEN DOVER
BOARD CERTIFIED
PROCTOLOGIST

LIFE IS CRAP®

It's true, life may not always
lay good fortune at your feet,

LIFE IS CRAP®

but don't worry, one day your ship will come in.

LIFE IS CRAP®

So remember,
when life knocks you down,

LIFE IS CRAP®

and throws you for a loop,

when it stinks,

LIFE IS CRAP®

or blows,

LIFE IS CRAP®

or bites,

LIFE IS CRAP®

or hurts,

LIFE IS CRAP®

just keep saying to yourself
life may be crap,

LIFE IS CRAP®

but at least we're all
in this crap together!